• PRACTICAL FISHKEEPING •

LIVE FOODS FOR AQUARIUM FISHES

John Rundle

John Rundle

RINGPRESS

ABOUT THE AUTHOR

John Rundle, a former marine engineer, now devotes himself
to breeding fish – a hobby he has enjoyed for more than 35
years. John writes regularly for *Practical Fishkeeping*
magazine, and is a well-respected lecturer. He works part-
time for the University of Plymouth, where he runs a
breeding programme for cuttlefish based at the Marine
Biological Association of the U.K.

SCIENTIFIC CONSULTANT: Dr. Peter Burgess BSc, MSc,
MPhil, PhD is an experienced aquarium hobbyist and
international consultant on ornamental fish.

Commercial products shown in this book are for illustrative
purposes only and are not necessarily endorsed by the author.

Photography: *John Rundle (p.9, p.10, p.11, p.15, p.17, p.18,*
p.21, p.23, p.26, p.28, p.31, p.37, p.40, p.42, p.49, p.50, p.52,
p.53 (Corydoras Panda), p.54, p.55. Mary Bailey (p.61),
Stan McMahon (p.35, p.44), Dr. David Ford (p.30, p.62),
Dr. Peter Burgess (p. 24, p. 41, p. 48), and courtesy of
Tetra UK. All other photos by Keith Allison.
Line drawings: Viv Rainsbury
Picture editor: Claire Horton-Bussey
Design: Rob Benson

Published by Ringpress Books,
a division of Interpet Publishing,
Vincent Lane, Dorking, Surrey, RH4 3YX, UK
Tel: 01306 873822   Fax: 01306 876712
email: sales@interpet.co.uk

First published 2002
© 2002 Ringpress Books. All rights reserved

ISBN 1 86054 260 3

Printed and bound in Hong Kong through
Printworks International Ltd.

10 9 8 7 6 5 4 3 2 1

CONTENTS

CHAPTER 1

WHAT ARE LIVE FOODS?

A diet which includes live food usually benefits a fish's colour and growth. Pictured: Clown loach (*Botia macracanthus*).

Fishkeepers have used live foods in some form or other since the birth of the fishkeeping hobby. Of course, it is now possible to keep aquarium fish alive by just feeding the vast range of modern dry foods such as flakes and granules. However, by using a combination of live and dry foods to form a varied, balanced diet, there is no doubt that the fish will benefit in their rate of growth and colour.

Live foods are an important source of proteins, vitamins and other nutrients, and retain active enzymes that make digestion more efficient for fish. All these factors help to make live foods a 'must' for feeding tiny fry and adults.

Fish breeders use live food to help condition prospective breeding stock, and, in some cases, certain species of aquarium fish will only eat food items if they are alive and moving.

SOURCES OF LIVE FOOD

Live foods fall into two categories:
• Cultured live foods
• Wild-collected foods.

It must be considered that, while wild-collected foods often have good nutritional value, some of them can host fish parasites, bacteria and viruses.

Feeding cultured live foods not only reduces the risk of disease, but using them is a very economical way of providing your fish with a steady supply of live prey organisms. It could be that the fishkeeper may have to travel some distance to collect live food from the wild, whereas cultured live foods can be harvested in the comfort of your own home.

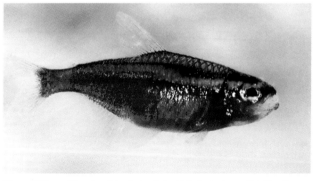

The addition of live food to their diet will help to keep fish like these in top condition. Pictured: a Cardinal Tetra (*Paracheirodon axelrodi*).

This book will cover practical methods on how to culture the popular range of live organisms for feeding adults, juveniles and fry. It will also look at a few of the popular wild-collected foods.

CULTURED FOODS

The procedures mentioned in this book are based on tried-and-tested methods and recipes used by the author, to successfully cultivate the following foods:

- Brine shrimp
- Grindal worm
- Infusoria
- Microworm
- Whiteworm.

The size of these foods varies from 25 mm (one inch) down to a few microns (one micron is a thousandth of a millimetre). The size of food is an important factor and must be considered for the size of the fish you intend to feed. Between them, cultured live foods can be used for feeding the full range of fish from adults down to tiny fry that may be only 1 mm in length.

WILD-COLLECTED FOODS

These are foods that can be collected from their natural environment and used to feed young and adult fish. The foods described are:

- Bloodworms
- *Daphnia*
- Earthworms
- *Gammarus*
- Gnat larvae.

There is a live food to suit all species and ages of fish. Pictured: Rainbowfish (*Glossolepis inciscus*).

TO BE AVOIDED

Tubifex is a well-known live food that can be bought in aquatic retail outlets, and maggots are normally sold as fishing bait. Both can cause problems when used to feed aquarium fish, as will be discussed later (see pages 61-62).

CHAPTER 2

WHITEWORMS

Whiteworms (*Enchytraeus albidus*) are segmented, round worms of about 20mm to 25mm ($^3/_4$-1 inch) in length, milky-white in appearance with bristly bodies. They are a popular cultured live food.

A brief look at the whiteworm classification shows that it is a member of the Annelida phylum, which contains more than 9,000 species. The annelids are divided into three classes, one of which is Oligochaeta, comprising approximately 3,250 species generally found living in the soil.

Whiteworms can be fed to all types of adult freshwater aquarium fish to help bring them into breeding condition. Pictured: Butterfly Cichlid (*Anomalochromis thomasi*).

Whiteworm should be fed as part of a varied menu.
Pictured: Black Widow Tetra (*Gymnocorymbus ternetzi*).

Moving on down the classification tree, its family is Enchytraeidae and the genus is *Enchytraeus*. They are hermaphroditic creatures, which means that functional reproductive organs of both sexes occur in the same individual. Reproduction is by cross-fertilisation.

USE OF WHITEWORMS

Whiteworms are an ideal food for juvenile and adult fish. Fed to juveniles, they will help achieve a good growth rate; for adult fish, whiteworms can be used to help stimulate breeding activity.

Compared with other live foods, such as *Daphnia* and *Tubifex*, whiteworms are said to contain 290 per cent more protein and 5 to 20 per cent more fats. Because of this possible high fat content, it is not wise to feed whiteworms every day. But used as part of a varied menu of foods, whiteworms provide an excellent supplementary source of nourishment.

STARTER CULTURES

A 'starter' culture will be needed to produce the main stock of whiteworms. These are advertised in *Practical Fishkeeping* magazine, or they can be obtained from fellow hobbyists.

When kept under the correct conditions, whiteworms can multiply at a fast rate. Within the first 4 weeks, the culture can triple in numbers, then, every 20 to 30 days, the population can increase several times. This fast rate of production means that only a small quantity of worms is initially required to start the culture off.

Masses of whiteworms.

CULTURE CONTAINER

A container will be needed to house the worms and the culture media. It is recommended that containers are not smaller than 30 cm length x 18 cm width x 13 cm depth (about 12 x 7 x 5 inches). The container material can be plastic or wood, both of which have been used successfully.

PLASTIC

Large ice cream containers or rectangular washing up bowls can be used. Plastic containers will obviously last for long periods of time, but they can make it difficult to control the moisture content of the culture medium.

WOOD

A long-lasting wood container can be made from 12-mm ($^1/_2$-in) thick wood. Wood also gives essential control over the moisture content.

COVERS

Covers for both of the materials, plastic or wood, can be made from 6-mm ($^1/_4$-in) thick wood. They must completely cover the containers, but should just rest on the top. This will help to contain moisture, but at the same time allow air to pass under the cover and allow the culture to breathe. Whiteworms are sensitive to light, as can be seen when harvesting worms with the cover off. In the light, they will soon disappear back into the culture compost.

Whiteworms have a high fat content, so should only be fed as an occasional treat. Pictured: Sailfin Molly (*Poecilia velifera*).

CULTURE MEDIA

There have been many types of compost used by fishkeepers for culturing whiteworms. The one successfully used by the author for many years consists of a blend of Irish moss peat, with good garden loam. Added to this is a small amount of aquarium gravel and perlite, a material used by gardeners which can be obtained at any garden centre. This will keep the compost loose and allow a good circulation of air.

The mixture comprises 40 per cent Irish moss peat, 50 per cent garden loam, 5 per cent aquarium gravel and 5 per cent perlite. Fill the container to about two-thirds of its depth with this mixture.

The ideal pH range of the culture media is 6.7 to 7. This can be checked using a standard garden soil test kit. A small amount of powdered chalk can be added to stop the medium becoming too acidic.

> **TOP TIP**
> **Do not use sedge peat; this will not stay fresh for long. Also, don't use commercial potting compost, as it could contain harmful chemicals.**

MOISTURE

Often, the failure of a culture can be put down to it having the incorrect moisture level within the media. It could be that it is too dry or just a soggy mess. The media must be kept just moist enough to maintain humidity – not only in the soil, but also in the atmosphere just above it.

Never pour water directly on to the culture; instead, use a plant mist-sprayer (that holds tapwater) to provide the correct moisture level. With experience, you

Feeding whiteworms will promote growth in juveniles. Pictured: a healthy adult Angelfish (*Pterophyllum scalare*).

will learn to gauge the correct level – the worms will soon let you know! If the medium is too wet, the worms tend to leave the container; if too dry, they will die. The worm has to have moisture in and around its body. Remember: the key word is 'moist' not wet.

TEMPERATURE

The optimum temperature range for reproduction is 15°C to 20°C (59°F to 68°F). At 9°C (48°F) whiteworms will stop reproducing, and they will start to die at 27°C (80°F). An ideal place to keep whiteworm cultures is in an unheated garage or shed. In the winter months, the cultures can be covered with towels to help maintain the temperature.

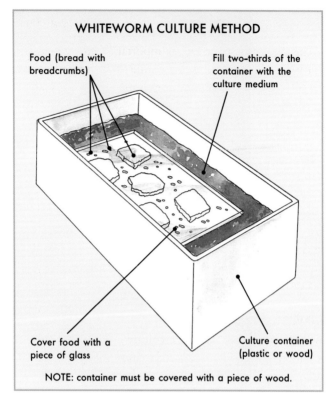

WHITEWORM CULTURE METHOD

Food (bread with breadcrumbs)

Fill two-thirds of the container with the culture medium

Cover food with a piece of glass

Culture container (plastic or wood)

NOTE: container must be covered with a piece of wood.

FEEDING THE CULTURE

There have been many recipes suggested for feeding these worms, some of which are a little bizarre. The foods mentioned here are tried and tested, and will provide good results. The ingredients are: white or brown bread, and wholemeal dry breadcrumbs that are used for cooking.

• Break the bread into pieces about 25 mm (1 inch) square and place on the surface of the compost.

• Add a sprinkling of breadcrumbs.

• Now place a piece of glass over the bread food. The glass sheet should be smaller than the culture container such that it does not completely cover the compost.

The amount you feed is an important factor when culturing whiteworms, and you must take into account the stage the culture is at. For example, if the culture is just starting, then only feed as much as the worms will eat within one day. Then increase the amount of food as the culture matures. A good benchmark is to start off with one piece of bread about 12 mm ($^1/_2$ inch) in diameter.

It is not uncommon for a good culture to clear a complete slice of bread within two days. Whatever the size of the culture, only feed a quantity of food that can be cleared within one to two days. Food that is uneaten after this time will start to attain growths of mould and this can turn the culture sour.

HARVESTING

Patience is required when the culture is first set up, so beware of the common fault of trying to harvest too early. It can take up to eight weeks before worms can be collected in numbers large enough to feed fish and

Once collected, the whiteworms will be received with relish.
Pictured: *Tetragonopterus argenteus* and *Pseudochalceus kyburzi*.

yet still sustain the culture. However, once the culture is at harvesting strength, it can last for a few months before the number of worms start to decline.

The harvesting procedure is as follows:

- Remove the piece of glass and scrape off the worms.
- Then harvest the packed worms from the top of the medium. An old kitchen knife is an ideal harvesting tool.
- Place the worms in a plastic tub that contains a small amount of water and leave for around five minutes. This allows the worms to purge any compost or food in their intestinal tract.
- By this time, the worms will have collected together in small balls. Decant off the surplus water, collect the worms using tweezers, and feed them to the fish.

NEW CULTURES

After some time, the culture will slow down in worm production; this will usually be caused by the compost becoming stale. A good sign of this is that the culture medium will become broken down by the worms into very fine particles. This will tend to cause it to pack and become sticky. When this happens, remove a small quantity of worms and use these to start a new culture with fresh compost.

A point worth noting is that whiteworm cultures do not take kindly to being disturbed too often, so do not stir up the medium every time you harvest them. Leave the medium alone until it needs replacing.

CHAPTER

3

GRINDAL WORMS

These cultured worms are found in the same genus as the whiteworm, with a Latin name of *Enchytraeus buccholzi*. Its common name, 'grindal worm' comes from a Swedish fishkeeper, Mrs Mortan Grindal, who first showed the fishkeeping world the practicability of culturing it as a valuable live fish food.

USE OF GRINDAL WORMS

The grindal worm is a small, white-coloured worm between 3 mm and 5 mm ($1/8$ inch to $3/16$ inch) in length, making it an excellent food for young and adult fish. Because fat and protein is lower in the grindal worm, it can be fed on a more regular basis than the larger and more nutritionally rich whiteworm (page 9). The grindal worm, like the whiteworm, is a hermaphrodite.

Grindal worm is an ideal food for growing on young fish. Pictured: A brood of young Dwarf Cichlids (*Apistogramma nijsseni*).

Grindal worms are slightly more difficult to culture than either whiteworm or microworm, but, if proper care is taken, they can be very prolific and reproduce rapidly.

STARTER CULTURES

To begin with, a starter culture will be required to establish the main breeding stock. As with whiteworms, these can be obtained through adverts in *Practical Fishkeeping* magazine or from friends who have a culture. Only a small quantity of worms is required to start the main stock culture.

CULTURE CONTAINERS

Small rectangular or round plastic containers are ideal to house the cultures. An example of the sizes used by the author are: 14 cm x 9 cm x 6 cm depth ($5^1/2$ in x $3^1/2$ in x $2^3/8$ in) or 15 cm diameter x 6 cm depth (6 in x $2^3/8$ in). Grindal worms prefer to be kept in the dark, so do not use transparent containers; old butter or margarine tubs are ideal for the job.

The containers must have fitting covers, each with a few small holes (about 2 to 3 mm – $1/8$ inch – in diameter) punched in to allow air circulation.

CULTURE MEDIA

Simply use moss peat, a material that can be found in any garden centre. Do not use sedge peat, as this does not stay fresh for as long as moss peat. Place the peat in the container to a depth of about 4 cm ($1^1/2$ in). There is no need to have a great depth of culture medium, because grindal worms live and feed on, or just under, the surface. On top of the peat, place a piece of glass

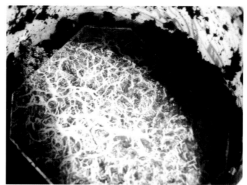

Grindal worms on the culture cover glass.

or clear plastic that covers about one half of the surface area. The worms will collect on the underside of the glass, making it easy for harvesting.

MOISTURE

The moisture content of the medium is critical in maintaining a good production rate of worms. The medium must be wet but not saturated; using a plant mist-sprayer to add the moisture is the best way to control this. Too dry and the worms will die, too wet and they will vacate the container.

TEMPERATURE

Grindal worm cultures must be kept warm to survive; ideal temperatures are around 23°C-26°C (73.5°F-78°F).

For fishkeepers with a heated fish house storing the cultures in a warm environment is not a problem. Alternatively, since the containers are quite small, they can be kept on the cover glass of a heated fish tank. This will maintain an adequate temperature for production. Another source of warmth could be near a greenhouse heater.

Do not keep the cultures in an area where food is prepared, such as a kitchen.

GRINDAL WORM CULTURE METHOD

1

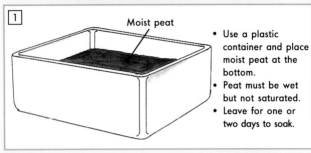

Moist peat

- Use a plastic container and place moist peat at the bottom.
- Peat must be wet but not saturated.
- Leave for one or two days to soak.

2

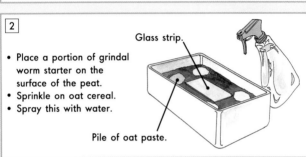

- Place a portion of grindal worm starter on the surface of the peat.
- Sprinkle on oat cereal.
- Spray this with water.

Glass strip.

Pile of oat paste.

3

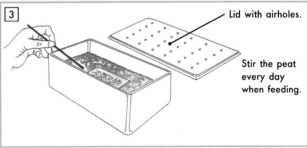

Lid with airholes.

Stir the peat every day when feeding.

4

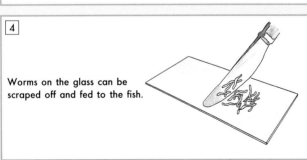

Worms on the glass can be scraped off and fed to the fish.

FEEDING THE WORMS

Feed grindal worms on instant oat cereal and baker's yeast granules.

- Place a few granules of yeast into a small amount of cold water, and allow them to disperse.
- Add a small amount of the oat cereal and mix into a creamy paste.
- Place the paste in small amounts on the surface of the compost. Three or four piles of about 12 mm (¹/2 inch) diameter will feed the culture.

When conditions are correct, the worms will soon devour the food and will require feeding twice a day. Just before you feed the worms, give the culture medium a good stir. This will stop it from compacting, and will allow air to circulate.

HARVESTING

It can take up to two weeks for a culture to establish and supply enough worms to harvest. It is wise to have more than one culture up and running, to allow for any problems that might cause a culture to crash.

Grindal worms contain less protein than Whiteworms, and can be fed on a more regular basis. Pictured: Pencilfish (*Nannobrycon eques*).

The worms will adhere to the underside of the cover glass. When you need to harvest the worms, just remove the cover glass and scrape off the amount required, using a small knife.

Make sure there is no culture medium or worm food attached to the collected worms. The worms can then be fed directly to the fish.

STARTING NEW CULTURES

Harvested daily, the cultures can last for up to three months, provided they are not kept too wet. When the number of worms being produced begins to drop, or the medium becomes sour, new cultures must be started. This can be done by taking a small amount of worms from the old culture and transferring them to a new one with fresh media.

MITES AND FLIES

While culturing whiteworms and grindal worms, there may be a time when very small black flies or mites (Springtails in the order Collembola) appear in the cultures. If this happens, they can be quickly eradicated by placing a few crystals of para-di-chlorobenzine on the surface of the culture medium in the corner of the container away from the worms. The crystals are sold to keep moths at bay on clothes; in fact, a very minute piece of a mothball will also work. It is a short-term operation, so has no harmful effect on the worms or fish.

CHAPTER

4

MICROWORMS

Microworms are an ideal first food for small fish, such as the Platy.
Pictured: adult Platy (*Xiphophorus maculatus*).

The microworm, a tiny, almost colourless nematode roundworm, can be found in various aquarium literature under different names such as: *Turbatrix aceti*, *Anguillula aceti*, *Anguillula silusia*, and, more recently, *Panagrellus silusae*.

The common name, 'microworm' is well suited, for it is less than 1 mm in length. It is so small that it is hard to distinguish a single worm with the naked eye; they are more easily seen as a mass. Their small size makes them a very good source of food for baby fish.

Microworms have an unusual method of reproducing – they are, in fact, livebearers. The greater percentage of the young worms will be females, so potentially the culture can rapidly increase in numbers.

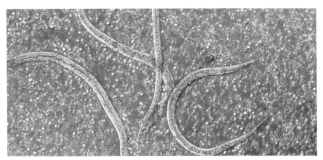
Close-up of microworms in culture medium.

USE OF MICROWORMS

The small size of this live food makes it ideal for feeding to very small aquarium fish fry. An example of a typical feeding pattern for fry would be to feed brine shrimp nauplii in the morning and then to feed microworms in the evening. Because of its minute size, it is not practical to feed microworms to adult fish.

CULTURE CONTAINERS

Small clear plastic containers about 10 cm (4 in) square or round are ideal to hold the cultures. They must have fitting lids with small holes to allow air to flow over the culture. By using clear containers, it is easier to sight and harvest the worms.

CULTURE METHOD

A starter culture can be obtained through adverts in *Practical Fishkeeping* magazine or through a fishkeeper friend.

Microworms are not cultured in a soil- or peat-based compost; they actually live in their own food. This food is instant oat cereal that is mixed with water. The paste should be of a consistency that will allow a matchstick to stand up of its own accord. The starter culture of microworms can now be added to this paste.

Now place enough of the brew into the plastic culture container (of about 10 cm x 10 cm – 4 in – in size) to a depth of 20 mm (^{3}/4 inch). Replace the lid of the container and put it in a warm environment around 23°C to 26°C (73.5°F to 78°F). Cooler temperatures are tolerated, however the worms will not reproduce so fast under cool conditions.

Within two days, the surface of the medium will be seen moving, and, by using a magnifying glass, hundreds of tiny worms will be observed.

HARVESTING AND RENEWAL

The worms should not be harvested until they are seen *en masse* climbing the sides of the container. Harvesting can be achieved by using a small artist's paintbrush to collect a mass of the worms from the container sides.

Feed directly to the fry or young fish by just swishing the brush in the tank; the very tiny worms will be seen as a cloud of dust in the water.

Do not dip the brush into the actual culture to collect microworms, as the culture medium could pollute the water and kill the fry.

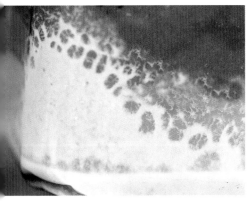

Microworms on the side of the container, ready to be harvested.

MICROWORM CULTURE

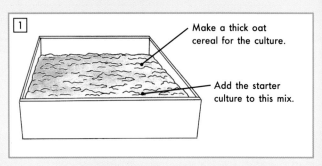

1. Make a thick oat cereal for the culture.

Add the starter culture to this mix.

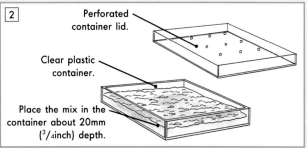

2. Perforated container lid.

Clear plastic container.

Place the mix in the container about 20mm (³/₄inch) depth.

3. Microworm will be seen climbing the sides.

Use an artist's paintbrush to harvest microworms from the sides.

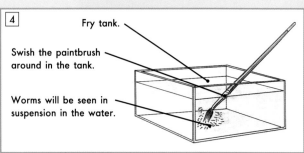

4. Fry tank.

Swish the paintbrush around in the tank.

Worms will be seen in suspension in the water.

Microworm is almost the same size as brine shrimp nauplii; making it an ideal food for tiny fry. You can keep a culture productive for up to two weeks. If it tends to dry a little, just damp the medium using a plant mist-sprayer.

Cultures that are going well have a slightly sweet smell: when they need renewing, the smell is not as sweet. At this stage, the number of worms seen climbing the container side will be less. Simply remove a small piece of the old culture to start a new one.

WHERE TO CULTURE

These worms need a source of warmth. If you do not have a fish house, the containers can be kept on the cover glass of a heated fish tank. This will maintain an adequate temperature for production. Another source of warmth could be near a greenhouse heater.

Do not keep any of the cultures in an area where food is prepared, such as a kitchen.

SUMMARY OF CULTURE WORM TECHNIQUES				
TYPE OF WORM	SIZE	CULTURE MEDIUM	CULTURE TEMPERATURE	FEED ENRICHMENT
Microworm	1 mm	Instant oat cereal	24°C to 27°C (75-81°F)	Instant oat cereal
Grindal worm	3 mm/ 5 mm	Moss peat	24°C to 27°C (75-81°F)	Instant oats cereal and breakfast cereal
Whiteworm	20 mm to 25 mm	Moss peat and garden loam	15°C to 20°C (59-68°F)	Bread and breadcrumbs

CHAPTER
5

BRINE SHRIMP

This relatively small crustacean has been used for feeding aquarium fish the world over since the early 1920s. Brine shrimp can be found living in salt lakes but not in the sea, and are distributed throughout the world, although the bulk of brine shrimp used by hobbyist fishkeepers come from North America.

The latin name of the brine shrimp is known generally as *Artemia salina*, though there are, in fact, about five different species.

Adult brine shrimps have the capability of producing hard-coated eggs, correctly known as cysts. These cysts can go into a resting period ('diapause') that can last for long periods of time, months or even years. It is this behaviour that allows them to be harvested and hatched

A male Ram Cichlid (*Microgeophagus ramirezi*) with a large brood of fry that will feed on brine shrimp nauplii.

by fishkeepers at a later date. These very tiny dry cysts can be bought and used as a very important source of live food for aquarium fish.

USE OF BRINE SHRIMP

It is the very small newly-hatched brine shrimp called a nauplius (plural: nauplii), that is used to feed fry, young fish and even some adult fish that may be stubborn feeders. In fact, when breeding fish, it is often imperative to use this source of live food to help raise broods of fry to adulthood.

If you do not want to hatch your own brine shrimp, it can be purchased from aquatic shops.

STORAGE

The dry cysts look like very fine brown grains. Correct storage of the cysts is of great importance. It can make all the difference between most of the cysts hatching or none at all.

The cysts do not like a damp atmosphere or extreme variables of temperature when in storage. They should be stored in a refrigerator and held in airtight containers. If possible, a sachet of silica gel desiccant should be placed in the container to keep the cysts free from moisture.

HATCHING METHOD

Ideally, use glass or firm plastic containers for hatching the brine shrimp. Coffee jars or bottles are fine for this purpose. The hatching success depends on three factors:

• Salinity
• Temperature
• Aeration.

Live adult brine shrimp.

SALINITY

To hatch brine shrimp, saline water is required. This can either be seawater or saline mix. With seawater, you must make sure that it is collected from an area free from pollution.

For the saline mix, the most common method is to mix a salt solution using either cooking salt, pure sea salt or marine salt (the latter sold for marine aquariums). Do not use table salt, as it contains additives for human digestion that may be harmful to fish. Mix the salt solution to a specific gravity of 1.020 at 24°C (75°F). You will need a hydrometer from the aquarium shop to measure specific gravity.

AERATION

This is crucial. The water in the hatching container must be aerated with a steady (not fierce) flow of air bubbles. An airline without an airstone should be inserted into the container, making sure that it reaches to the bottom. You will therefore need an air pump.

The movement of the water will stop the cysts from collecting at the base of the container, and the air itself is necessary as the thousands of tiny live shrimp would otherwise soon die if no air were supplied.

TEMPERATURE

Temperature is a controlling factor on the time it takes the cysts to hatch. At a temperature between 27°C (80°F) and 28°C (82°F) the cysts will hatch in 24 hours. At lower temperatures, the hatching time will take longer. Do not incubate below 21°C (70°F).

HATCHING AMOUNTS

Because of the high cost of brine shrimp cysts, care must be taken not to waste them by hatching more nauplii than you need. Also, use the hatched nauplii as soon as possible, as they will not live for long periods of time if left in the freshwater when harvested (see Harvesting, below).

It has been calculated that there are about 300,000 brine shrimp cysts per gram (0.035oz); this provides a benchmark for assessing the requirement.

The nauplii form is generally used to feed fry and young fish.
Pictured: group of young Pigmy Catfish (*Corydoras pygmaeus*).

BRINE SHRIMP HATCHING METHOD

1

Air supply
(from air pump).

Hatching container
(large coffee jar).

At a temperature of 27°C
to 28°C, eggs will hatch
within 24 hours.

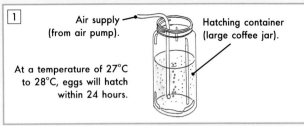

2

1. Handkerchief placed over a plastic container.

2. Only the saltwater passes through.

3. Contents of hatching container poured into the handkerchief.

4. Brine shrimp will be trapped in the handkerchief.

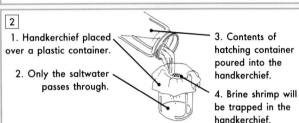

3 Prepare a container with *fresh* water not *salt* water. Use a 6"x 6" x 6" (15.5cm square) glass tank, or thereabouts.

Fresh water

< 6" > < 6" >

6"

4 1. Take the handkerchief and disperse the contents (brine shrimps and shells) into the water.

3. Remove live brine shrimp for feeding with a small syringe or pipette.

2. Use a light to attract the shrimp. Egg shells will remain on the tank floor.

5 Pour the salt water back into the hatching container and add more cysts.

HARVESTING

To harvest newly-hatched brine shrimp:

- Fill a small container with tap water. (The author uses a small glass tank, 15 cm/6 in square.)
- Place a handkerchief over a large, clean coffee jar, or use a brine shrimp net (available from aquarium shops).
- Remove the airline from the hatching jar and pour the contents over the handkerchief.
- The salt water will filter through, leaving live nauplii and cyst shells trapped in the handkerchief.
- To separate the live shrimp from the shells, the contents of the handkerchief can be placed in the container of fresh water.
- The young shrimp are attracted to light. By placing a light source, such as a torch or electric light, near the base of the tank, the shrimp will move towards it.
- They will collect in a pink mass and can be removed by means of a pipette or a small syringe.
- The empty cyst shells will float on the surface away and hence won't contaminate the nauplii that are gathering at the base of the tank. Ensure that no empty cyst shells are added to the fry tank, as the tiny fry have serious problems digesting the hard shell cases.

RECYCLING

After cleaning the hatching container, the salt water can be poured back into it and the cycle will start again when fresh cysts are added. The salt water can be used for about four days before it will need renewing.

ADULT SHRIMPS

It is possible to grow the freshly-hatched brine shrimp

naplii to adult stage. This valuable source of live food can be used to feed young and adult fish. To do this, it is necessary to examine the brine shrimp in more detail before looking at the methods used to grow them on.

SHRIMP DEVELOPMENT

During its development from nauplius to adult, the brine shrimp will go through various stages called 'instars'. At each stage or instar the brine shrimp will moult. The number of moults depends on factors such as salinity and temperature. At a specific gravity (SG) of 1.085 and a temperature of 22°F, up to 12 to 16 moults has been counted with the San Francisco Bay shrimp. The typical first three stages of moulting and growth are as follows.

STAGE 1

Upon emergence from the cyst, the size of the naplii is 0.32 mm ($^1/_8$ inch). After 24 hours, it will moult and enter the next stage.

Adult brine shrimp can be fed to a wide variety of fish, including the Tiger Scat (*Scatophagus*) which is mainly vegetarian.

Adult male brine shrimp.

STAGE 2

Its size now is 0.63 mm ($^1/_4$ inch). Within another 24 hours, it will moult and enter the next stage.

STAGE 3

Its size now is 0.90 mm.

With each moult, the young shrimps alter in body shape and in nutritional comparison. Growth and development generally ends in 12 to 14 days at a final adult size of about 6.5 mm ($^1/_4$ inch) for San Francisco Bay brine shrimp.

It should be noted that the newly-hatched brine shrimp is very nutritious, being rich with yolk from the cyst. It is this yolk that sustains it until it develops its mouth and begins feeding. Within 24 to 35 hours, the nutritional value diminishes as the shrimps draw on their fatty acid reserves. This is why newly-hatched brine shrimp nauplii should be used as soon as possible. Any remaining after 24 hours should be discarded or grown on.

GROWING ON

Over the years, hobbyist fishkeepers have used various methods and recipes all with varying degrees of success. The author uses an easily-obtained food for the shrimp, and describes his growing-on method here.

GROWING-ON CONTAINER

Small glass fish tanks make ideal containers for this project, the size of which depends on how many adult brine shrimp are required.

There are figures quoted for the density of shrimp that can be raised per volume of water in the container. One often-quoted figure is two shrimp per millilitre of water (i.e. 2,000 shrimp per litre). This would suggest that a tank of, say, 60 cm x 30 cm x 30 cm (23.5 in x 12 in x 12 in) filled to a depth of 20 cm (8 in) that holds 36.6 litres (8.2 gal) of water would hold 73,000 brine shrimp.

The author has found this to be high and instead recommends a quarter of this number (i.e. about 18,000 shrimps per 36.6 litres of water).

Note: do not hatch the cysts in the growing-on tank.

WATER

Salt water is required and this can be obtained the same way as for hatching the cysts. Brine shrimp are quite hardy, and have been known to survive in water with salinity in excess of eight times that of normal seawater.

The salinity for growing on is around 1.050 SG; this is higher than for hatching the cysts. By topping up with distilled water, or tapwater left to stand for 24 hours, it is possible to compensate for any water loss caused by evaporation and the resulting rise in salinity.

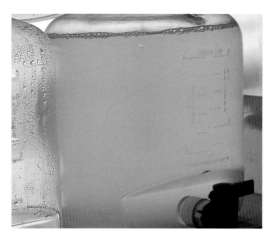

Algae culture
for feeding
brine shrimp.

FOOD

Brine shrimp are filter feeders, which means they
require very minute foods hence. Hence to grow on
brine shrimp, their food must have a particulate size
within the range of 6 to 15μm (μ=micrometre). A
micrometre is one-millionth of a metre.

In their natural environment, they feed on a species
of phytoplankton algae called *Dunaliella sauna*. Because
it is often not possible for hobbyist fishkeepers to
culture *Dunaliella*, other sources of foods have been
used to grow on the shrimp. These include yeast, dried
rice bran, and green water. All of these require
preparation and have varying degrees of success.

The food recommended in this book is 'Marine
Liquify', a commercial product sold as a liquid food for
filter feeders and other plankton feeders in marine
aquariums. It can easily be obtained from any aquatic
retail outlet. There are other brine shrimp foods that
are also commercially available.

TEMPERATURE

Aim for a temperature between 25 to 27°C (77-81°F).

AERATION

Do not use filtration, only low-level aeration. An open-ended airline (no airstone), producing a steady flow of bubbles that does not cause severe water turbulence, is all that is required.

LIGHTING

Brine shrimp can be grown on using lighting or in darkness, depending on the type of food used. If phytoplankton algae (green water) are used, then some form of direct lighting regime is needed, such as a 40-watt cool white fluorescent tube that is on a continuous light cycle. Lighting is not required if using such foods as the yeast, rice bran or the marine fry food recommended in this book.

GROWING-ON METHOD

A tank 60 cm x 30 cm x 30 cm (23.5 in x 12 in x 12 in) is filled to a depth of 20 cm (8 in) with salt water. An open-ended airline is placed in the tank, together with a heaterstat. A smaller tank can be used depending on how many adult shrimp is required.

There is no specific lighting set-up for this method. In fact, the tank is covered to keep light out. The only area that lets direct light in is the front glass of the tank. Do not use gravel or any other substrate.

Now add the newly-hatched brine shrimp nauplii, and feed them using commercial marine fry food. Do not pour neat fry food directly into the tank. Shake the bottle well and mix some in a container that holds a small amount of tank water.

Use two drops of the liquid food per 4.5 litres (1 gallon) of tank water. Mix this solution well and

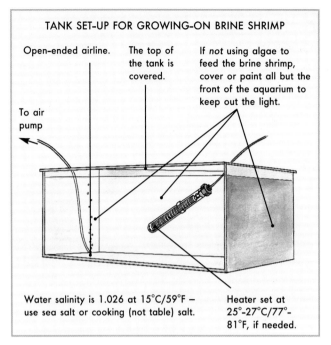

TANK SET-UP FOR GROWING-ON BRINE SHRIMP

Open-ended airline.

The top of the tank is covered.

If *not* using algae to feed the brine shrimp, cover or paint all but the front of the aquarium to keep out the light.

To air pump

Water salinity is 1.026 at 15°C/59°F – use sea salt or cooking (not table) salt.

Heater set at 25°-27°C/77°-81°F, if needed.

pour into the tank. The water will cloud slightly.

Using this method, only one partial water change of 25 per cent is required during the 14 to 15 days of brine shrimp growth. However, distilled water (or tap water that has been left standing for 24 hours) may need to be added to adjust the salinity, where necessary.

The brine shrimp will clear the water within 2 to 3 days. Once this happens, feed them again. They will reach adult size in about 14 days.

CHAPTER

6

INFUSORIA

This minute, but very valuable live food has caused problems for many fishkeepers in terms of what is it and how it is cultured. The definition of infusoria found in a biology dictionary is: "A term formerly applied to microscopic organisms found in infusions of organic substances". From this, we can deduce that it is a life-form and it is minute. In fact, it is so tiny that a microscope is required to see infusoria clearly as individuals.

They are, in fact, protozoa – animal organisms that consist only of one cell. One group of protozoa is the Ciliates and these form the basis of infusoria cultures. All the species in this group have thread-like appendages or cilia that move in a wavelike motion.

Infusoria is an ideal first food for very tiny fry, such as the Black Ruby Barb (*Barbus nigrofasciatus*). Pictured: an adult Black Ruby.

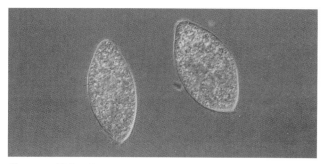
Close-up of infusoria organisms.

This provides a means of propulsion and also produces water currents to gather food into the ciliates 'mouth'.

One of the well-known Ciliates is *Paramecium*. It is called the 'Slipper Animal' because of its elongated shape, and is often mentioned in fishkeeping literature as a source of food for feeding tiny fry.

USE OF INFUSORIA

The key word is 'size'. For example: newborn guppy or platy fry are about 4 mms ($^1/_8$ inch) in length, and are immediately able to take foods such as crushed dry flake food or live brine shrimp nauplii. On the other hand, the very minute fry of species of egglayers (like tetras, barbs, danios, rasboras and gouramies) may only be 1.5 mm ($^1/_{16}$ inch) in length or less. So imagine the size of the mouths of these fry – they are far too small to take brine shrimp or crushed dry foods. To match the tiny size of the fry, you require a tiny live food source – in this case, 'infusoria'.

CULTURING INFUSORIA

In the wild, fish will find and feed on 'infusion type' foods within their natural environment. In the case of tetras, which live in small streams and rivers, these waters will flood in the rainy season, prompting the fish

A cloud of infusoria.

to spawn. Submerged dead leaves and grasses will encourage the proliferation of minute infusoria-type life forms that the resulting fish fry feed on.

Hobbyist fish breeders simulate these conditions by substituting clean, fresh water for the rain to trigger spawning, and then use infusoria cultures to supply the resultant fry with food.

Over the years, there have been many suggested recipes for producing infusoria, such as hay or straw, potato, turnip, lettuce and commercial products. Some will produce good cultures and others will produce an odious smelling brew. (The author has tried all of them.)

What follows is the material and method the author has used for years with great success. It provides a good, clean infusoria culture to feed tiny fry.

CULTURE CONTAINER
Use two small, clear plastic or glass tanks 18 cm x 15 cm x 15 cm (7 in x 6 in x 6 in). You can, of course, use larger tanks, but do not go below the sizes mentioned.

TEMPERATURE
A constant temperature of 23°C to 24°C (73°F to 75°F) should produce infusoria within four days. The lower the temperature, the longer the culture takes to develop. Do not go below 21°C (70°F).

INFUSORIA CULTURE METHOD

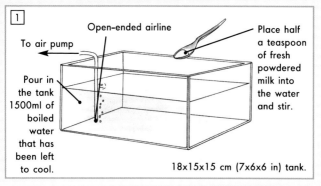

1

Open-ended airline

To air pump

Place half a teaspoon of fresh powdered milk into the water and stir.

Pour in the tank 1500ml of boiled water that has been left to cool.

18x15x15 cm (7x6x6 in) tank.

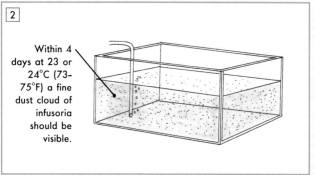

2

Within 4 days at 23 or 24°C (73-75°F) a fine dust cloud of infusoria should be visible.

METHOD OF CULTURE

- Pour 1500 ml or 2 pints of cold water into one of the tanks. Allow this to reach the required temperature.
- Place an open-ended airline into the tank, and set it to produce a medium flow of air bubbles.
- Place a level half-teaspoon of fresh powdered milk into the water, and stir it. The water will cloud to some extent at this stage.
- At the suggested temperature, the water will clear within four days, and fine dust-like clouds of infusoria can be seen. If a light source is placed by

the side of the tank the infusoria will be drawn to it and collect *en masse*. This is a good way of telling the density of the culture.

- Now start the second culture; this way, two cultures can give a continuous supply.
- From the time the water clears, the culture will last for about five days. Of course, this will also depend on how much infusoria you are using to feed the fry.
- It is possible to sustain the culture for longer periods by stirring in just a further pinch of powdered milk. Do not add too much powdered milk, as you will only produce a smelly mess that is of no use for feeding fish.

FEEDING

Do not attempt to feed the fry before they are free-swimming. This is when they have used up their food supply in the yolk sac and can actually be seen swimming in the water column.

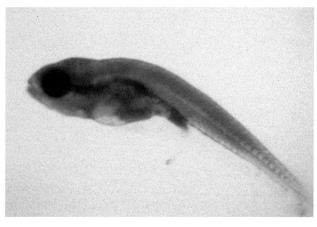

This tetra fry is 2 mm in length. Its first food would be infusoria.

The fry of egglayers, like this Diamond Tetra (*Moenkhausia pitteri*), have tiny mouths and can only cope with minute infusoria. Adult fish pictured.

The amount of infusoria to feed is difficult to quantify, it is a question of finding a balance. Too little, and the fry may starve; too much, and tank water may become polluted (and the fry will die).

The factors that govern the quantity are:
• Size of tank.
• Size of brood.

About 200 ml of a rich infusoria culture will feed a brood of, say, 150 Glowlight Tetra fry. The breeding tank will be in the region of 46 cm x 20 cm x 30 cm (18 in x 8 in x 12 in). These 200 ml will feed the brood until they are of a size to take the next food that would be brine shrimp nauplii.

Use this as a benchmark and adjust it to suit the size of tank and the brood size of any fish that you are breeding. Remember that the fry should not have to search for infusoria, it must be in sufficient quantities almost to swim into their tiny mouths!

Adult Glowlight Tetra. Infusoria is an ideal food for the fry of this species.

WHICH FISH REQUIRE INFUSORIA?

There is no easy answer to this question. Although the great majority of aquarium fish fry will eat infusoria, if their mouths are large enough to take larger foods (such as brine shrimp or microworm) as their first food, then there's little point giving them infusoria.

Here is a general list of recommended first foods for various groups of tropical aquarium fish:

Brine Shrimp or Microworm:	Infusoria:
• Dwarf Cichlids	• Tetras
• Angels	• Barbs
• Catfish	• Gouramis
• Livebearers	• Danios
• Medium to large Killifish	• Rasboras
• All varieties of goldfish.	• Small Killifish.

CHAPTER

7

DAPHNIA

Daphnia is a small crustacean, commonly called the water-flea because it makes jerky, jumping movements. *Daphnia* has always been a popular live food used by fishkeepers to feed tropical and coldwater fish.

Daphnia is a very versatile food suitable for coldwater and tropical species, such as Lionhead goldfish and Red shiners (*Cyprinella lutrensis*, above) and Angelfish, (*Pterophyllum scalare*, below).

DAPHNIA BIOLOGY

Daphnia is the genus name, and there are many species that can be found the world over and in different living conditions. In Europe, *Daphnia pulex* is the species most commonly found and used as a fish food. A related group of water-fleas of the genus *Moina* are used to feed ornamental fish in south-east Asia and elsewhere.

Daphnia are especially abundant during the spring and summer months. They are found in ponds and lakes rich in various small organisms such as bacteria, algae and protozoa, upon which they feed. Digestion of these foods is rapid, in fact the food may remain in the gut of the water-flea for only half an hour.

Normally the colour of *Daphnia* is pinkish-brown, but you will also find them bright red in colour; this is when they multiply to excess and they start to deplete the dissolved oxygen in the water. This red colour is due to large amounts of haemoglobin that the *Daphnia* produces in its blood when in poorly-oxygenated conditions. When transferred to well-aerated water, the amount of haemoglobin in its blood decreases and the *Daphnia* resumes its normal body colour.

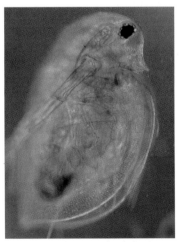

Daphnia are particularly abundant in spring and summer.
Pictured: close-up of *Daphnia*.

Daphnia are found in nutrient-rich ponds that harbour small organisms.

SUMMER FEMALES

A female *Daphnia* lays her eggs into a brood pouch situated within the hind part of her outer transparent shell. In this pouch, the female stores and hatches her summer eggs, which can take up to two to four days to hatch. When the young are liberated, they are fully-formed miniature adults. Soon after liberating a brood, the female moults and then lays another batch of eggs into the brood pouch. Summer eggs always develop into females, and several generations of all-female *Daphnia* can be produced over summer, without the presence of a male.

WINTER MALES

But with the approach of the colder months of autumn and winter, fertile males make their appearance in every brood. These males fertilise the winter eggs that are enclosed in a protective case called the ephippium. The ephippium is released at the time of a late seasonal moult and eggs contained in it remain dormant until the following spring or a spell of mild weather.

Then, with a rise in water temperature and a change in day length, the eggs hatch and a new batch of females appear to restart the cycle as before.

Although *Daphnia* can be fed to all types of fish, coldwater fishkeepers use it in large quantities to achieve good growth in their stock. Pictured: Bristol Shubunkins.

COLLECTING DAPHNIA

To collect this live food, you will need a fairly large fine-meshed net, preferably with a long handle, and a large container with a lid. Use a light-coloured container so you can easily inspect its contents.

When fishing for live food, seek the pond owner's permission, where necessary, and do not collect from conservation areas.

A figure-of-eight movement through the water with the net should collect a large quantity of *Daphnia* if the pond is rich in these crustaceans.

Do not collect more than you can use and do not overcrowd your container, otherwise the *Daphnia* will not make the journey home. Once you get them home, place them into fresh, cool tapwater.

It is possible that you will net other pond life along with the *Daphnia*, such as water boatman, water beetles and other creatures, including fish parasites such as the fish-louse (*Argulus*). Possibly these can be removed with a small net after first placing all the collection into a white container (such as a washing-up bowl).

As an alternative to catching your *Daphnia*, you can buy small bags of live ones from aquarium shops. It is an easier way of obtaining them; however, one bag will only feed a small number of fish.

CULTURING DAPHNIA

Small cultures of *Daphnia* can be maintained outdoors without too much trouble during the spring and summer. Of course, the size of the container used to hold the culture will determine its potential yield, but do not use anything smaller than a washing-up bowl.

Daphnia can be cultured outdoors if indoor space is at a premium.
Pictured: Gold Gouramis (*Trichogaster trichopterus*).

Large high-sided water butts (e.g. as used for collecting rain water from the roof) make good culture containers.

It is advisable to keep your culture containers raised off the ground; this will stop frogs and newts from entering the water.

FEEDING THE CULTURE

There are many successful recipes suggested for feeding the *Daphnia*, all of which are based on producing algae (green water) or micro-organisms upon which the *Daphnia* feed. These algae or micro-organisms should be allowed to build up, prior to seeding the container with a starter culture of *Daphnia*.

The following types of organic matter can be used:
• Baker's yeast
• Garden soil
• Dried grass
• Powder soya bean
• Dried horse manure.

Always introduce these foods sparingly, and make sure the garden soil and the dried grass have not been in contact with pesticides. Or you can directly feed the *Daphnia* by adding green water, from an ornamental pond, for example.

CHAPTER
8

BLOODWORMS

Bloodworms are the larvae of the non-biting midge *Chironomus*. They are very nutritious and are highly regarded as a live food for aquarium fishes. Bloodworms are rich in protein and provide a good source of iron for the fish, since they contain haemoglobin in their blood.

Live bloodworms.

BLOODWORM BIOLOGY
There are four stages in the life of the bloodworm: egg, larva, pupa and adult midge. Each midge can lay an egg mass in the water that contains between 50 to 700 eggs. Hatching time varies between 24 and 48 hours, depending on the temperature.

On hatching, the larvae are 1 mm ($^{1}/_{25}$ in) long, but grow up to 15 mm ($^{5}/_{8}$ in) before reaching the pupal stage. It is the larvae that are devoured by fish.

COLLECTING BLOODWORMS
Bloodworms can be found in bodies of water with muddy or silted bottoms, such as natural ponds, or even in the bottom of water butts. To collect bloodworm, the mud from the bottom must first be netted in a fine mesh net.

Corydoras Catfish, such as these *Corydoras panda*, love to search for live bloodworms on the base of the aquarium.

The contents are then passed through a sieve, to wash away the fine mud. The larvae and the coarse particles of detritus will remain in the sieve and are rinsed in a bucket of clean water. The bloodworms can then be caught with a net.

Small bags of live bloodworm can sometimes be obtained from aquatic shops. This is obviously an easier way of obtaining them; however, one bag will only feed a small number of fish. Bloodworms are cultured in large numbers in the Far East to feed fish on the commercial fish farms. In cooler climates, they are seasonally available.

Bloodworm is a very nutritious live food. Pictured: Rainbowfish feeding on bloodworm.

CHAPTER

9

MISCELLANEOUS LIVE FOODS

GNAT LARVAE

In their natural habitats, many of the fish we keep in our tanks would feed on various types of fly larvae. In the tropics, it would be the mosquito larvae, and copious amounts of this live food would be available. In Europe, it is the larvae of the common

Live gnat larvae.

gnat (*Culex pipens*) that can be collected to feed fish.

Black in colour, and about 7 mm ($^1/_3$ in) in length, gnat larvae can be found during spring and summer in still bodies of water, hanging head down suspended from the surface of the water. They can also be found in uncovered water butts and fish-free ponds. They are commonly known as wrigglers, because, when disturbed, they quickly leave the surface and travel downwards with a wriggling movement. However, they quickly return to the surface as they rely on atmospheric air to breathe.

COLLECTING GNAT LARVAE

Once on the surface, they can be netted without too much of a problem before they make a dash for the

Fish that feed in the top areas of the aquarium, such as the Danio (*Danio pathirana*) will take gnat larvae from the surface.

bottom of the area of water they are living in. Release the captured larvae into a container of clean water; from here they can be fed directly to the fish.

GAMMARUS

This small crustacean, known as the freshwater shrimp (*Gammarus pulex*), is usually found in shallow running water. It can be collected all year round from beds of aquatic vegetation. By shaking the water plants over a sheet of plastic, the shrimps will fall on to the sheet, and can then be transferred to a container holding clean water.

The adults are about 17 mm (^{11}/16 in) in length. Among the collection, smaller young shrimps will be found – exact replicas of the adults.

Note: Gammarus have a tough outer shell, making them suitable only for large fish.

EARTHWORMS

The common earthworm (*Lumbricus terrestris*) is used by fishkeepers to feed large species of tropical fish, such as large cichlids, and also for common and fancy goldfish. In fact, it is recognised by many top goldfish breeders as being one of the best foods for bringing goldfish into breeding condition.

Even better are smaller red worms (*Bimastrus foetida* and *Lumbricus rubellus*) that are up to 60 mm (2³/₈ in) in length and which can be found alongside the common earthworm.

Avoid the large worms known as the dung worm (*Eisenia foetida*), as these tend to be tough and not easily digested by fish. These worms are easily identified by their yellow colour.

COLLECTING THE WORMS

A successful collecting method is to lay a piece of material (such as sacking) on the ground. Keep the material damp and place some old tea leaves under it. This will encourage worms to gather under the cloth so that they can be easily collected. Do not collect earthworms from soils that have been treated with pesticides.

FEEDING TO THE FISH

The selected worms should be washed in clean water to remove any surplus soil or mud. Small worms up to 15 mm (⁵/₈ in) long can be fed directly to largish fish. If longer, they should be chopped into suitable lengths – a job that is not relished by some fishkeepers!

Earthworms are ideal for coldwater species, such as Goldfish. Pictured: Fantail goldfish.

FOOD SUMMARY SELECTION CHART

FOOD	ADULTS	FRY	AVAILABILITY	REMARKS
Infusoria		X	Cultured	First food for many egglayer fry
Microworm	X	X	Cultured	New born livebearer fry, and Cichlids will take this food
Grindal worm	X	X	Cultured	
Whiteworm			Cultured	Only feed once or twice a week
Brine shrimp nauplii		X	Hatched from cysts	First food for many types of fish or second food after infusoria
Daphnia			Collected or bought in small quantities	Risk of importing disease
Gnat larvae	X	X	Collected	Found only in spring and summer
Bloodworm	X	X	Collected or bought in small quantities	Good food for bottom feeders
Earthworms	X		Collected	Do not use if pesticides have been used on the soil
Gammarus	X		Collected	For large fish

X = Suitable.

CHAPTER

10

CONTROLLING THE DIET

This book does not cover the complete range of live foods that can be fed to aquarium fish. It covers what the author considers to be the top ten live foods that can be easily obtained and used by fishkeepers.

As part of a varied diet, these foods will help to condition fish to breed and feed the resulting fry. Or they could be used to feed those problem fish that will not take to eating dry or inanimate foods.

All fish benefit from a varied, nutritious diet. Pictured: Tiger Barbs.

FEEDING QUANTITIES

Care must be taken in the quantity of live food that is fed. When feeding the cultured worms such as microworm, grindal worm and whiteworm, do not over feed. These worms will die after being in water for some length of time, so remove any excess or dead worms left by the fish.

Brine shrimp nauplii will also die if left in freshwater, so only feed the amount that the fish will clear in a short time. Dead brine shrimp in a tank of fry can cause disease and pollution problems, and hence kill your fry.

Care must be also taken with other live foods, such as *Daphnia*, gnat larvae and bloodworm. These foods will stay alive for long periods of time; in fact, the gnat larvae and bloodworm will change into their flying adult stage if allowed.

If fed in very large numbers, *Daphnia* can use up the oxygen needed by the fish, so only give the amount of food that will be eaten in one feed.

FEEDING PATTERNS

When and how often to feed the foods is an important factor to consider. Here are some typical feeding regimens that you may find useful.

FEEDING FRY

In the case of tetra, barb, and danio fry, feed infusoria for 5-14 days (depending on the species). Then feed brine shrimp in the morning and microworm in the evening.

Danio fry do well on brine shrimp and microworm.
Pictured: Giant Danio (*Danio aequipinnatus*).

FEEDING YOUNG TROPICAL FISH
Feed grindal worms in the morning, and dry foods in the afternoon.

FEEDING ADULTS
All the foods recommended for adult fish in the table on page 57 (with the exception of whiteworm) can be fed daily as part of a dry/live food diet.

Whiteworms are an excellent clean source of live food, but they have quite a high fat content. Because of this, they should be fed only once or twice a week.

FOODS TO AVOID
MAGGOTS
Owners of large fish use maggots to feed their fish. These can be bought from fishing-tackle shops where they are sold as bait. What must be avoided are the coloured maggots. These are artificially coloured with various dyes to attract fish. All maggots are very fatty so use sparingly, if at all.

Large species, such as the *Parachromis managuensis* cichlid, can be fed the occasional maggot.

TUBIFEX

These small, red-coloured worms were once a main
source of live food, for all types of aquarium fish.
Nowadays, *Tubifex* is not used so often, because it is
known to carry fish parasites and pathogens.

The worms are commonly found living in the mud of
very polluted waters; they were collected in vast
quantities up to the late 1980s to supply the aquarium
hobby. Since then, many of the rivers have been cleaned
up, thus reducing the number of collection sites.
However, *Tubifex* is still sometimes available in aquarium
shops. When there are so many alternative foods to use,
why take the risk? The best advice is to avoid *Tubifex*.

PREPARING WILD-COLLECTED FOODS

To reduce the risk of introducing any disease problems
into the aquarium, it is possible to partly disinfect certain
live food organisms (e.g. *Daphnia*, gnat larvae and
Gammarus) collected from the wild.

There are commercial aquatic medications that can be
used for this purpose, or use a very weak 1 per cent
stock solution of potassium permanganate. The foods
are placed in a bowl or small tank of clean water and
treated for about 5 to 10 minutes. This procedure will
only reduce the risk of disease problems, as it will not
kill pathogens living in the tissues or gut of the live food.

FROZEN LIVE FOODS

It is now possible to buy blister or foil packs of frozen
Tubifex, *Daphnia*, bloodworm, and brine shrimp. These
frozen forms of food have several advantages. They are
available all year round, they are easy to store, and are
virtually disease-free (especially gamma-irradiated forms

Wild-collected live foods should always be cleaned before giving them to your fish. Pictured: Angelfish, *Pterophyllum scalare.*

The disadvantages of frozen live food include:
- Expense
- Slightly less nutritious than their living counterparts
- Immobile, so will not be taken by those fish and fry that will only feed on living, moving foods.

Frozen bloodworms, glassworms, brine shrimps, and *Daphnia*.

VARIED DIETS

To conclude, one point that must be noted is that no single species of live food should be fed exclusively. This is because each live food species is limited in its composition of essential nutrients, and its sole use may result in the fish developing nutritional deficiency problems. Instead, feed a range of live foods in addition to dry foods, so as to achieve a healthy and varied diet.

Fed as part of a varied diet, live foods can give fish an unmistakable healthy appearance. Pictured: Pearl Lace Gourami (*Trichogaster leeri*).